# THE GHOST OF THE SUNDANCE KID AND OTHER STORIES

## Biblical Parapsychology ™

June Raleigh

# CONTENTS

# CHAPTER 1

## The Ghost of the Sundance Kid

The reason I am writing this for him is because I have a photograph of his ghost. This picture was taken inside the actual cabin he lived in off and on, the same one you see on the front cover. It is not the first time I have photographed a ghost, 1. but when this occurs I always follow through with a story for the person who is appearing because they want something. I believe he wants a few things revealed.

I am not a ghost hunter and am not fascinated by death, because God hates death, and I figure we'll all find out about it soon enough anyway. The thing is a ghost picture is a special event and I am respectful regarding it.

As you can see there is a phantom type face superimposed on the framed antique picture. At first I had no clue who this was but after comparing the expression and the facial features, especially the dominant eye and shape of the face with many men in diverse photographs it became evident that this is the face of Harry Alonzo Longabaugh, who is famously known as the Sundance Kid. There is a shirt collar below the face and what looks like a silver bolo tie in a diamond shape. Here is a similar tie:

bolo tie

Harry Alonzo Longabaugh

At first glance the eye looks fuzzy and darkish but his actual right eye is sharp and connected just to the right of the fuzzy eye-when you find it you will see he is looking directly at you with a steady gaze.

I was not looking for ghosts, just taking tourist type pictures of the old Hole in the Wall cabin. This is the actual cabin that the Sundance Kid and the cold-blooded lawman killer Harvey Logan, alias Kid Curry lived in when they were planning a holdup of the bank in Red Lodge, Wyoming. It was moved from its original location (below) to Cody, Wyoming and is now part of a tourist attraction there called "Old Trail Town."

Pertaining to Harvey Logan, these two men were not alike, only to the extent they committed crimes together. A hardened criminal, Logan had no reservations about killing while Sundance, although he shot two Pinkerton pursuers while fleeing never killed anyone. Lawmen eventually caught up with Logan in 1904 in Parachute, Colorado after Logan had taken part in a train hold-up on June 7th. After a two day pursuit he shot and killed himself rather than being taken prisoner on June 9th.

The gun Harry used was a .45 Long Colt, a Single Action Army revolver with a 5 ½ inch barrel called the "Artillery Model." To the left of his face in the ghost photo is Harry's gun almost pointing at me as I take the picture and there is a faint outline of a trigger. The white (ivory) handle or stock is to the left, the lock is attached to it, but you can't see the length of the barrel because he's aiming his gun nearly straight into the camera. There is a small vertical white light at the barrel's end as though a bullet was being fired out of it, or perhaps residual smoke.

Here is a sample gun pictured below similar to the one he used in life with a 5 ½ inch barrel:

The average price of a gun like this one sold for about $17.00 in the 1870's.

The Sundance Kid once said "There is only one reason to carry a gun, and that is to kill a man." Ironically he never did. To corroborate the gun revealed in the ghost picture, shortly after the Union Pacific Train robbery in 1899 (which we will describe in detail below), Harry was seen in the Roundhouse Saloon in Linwood, Utah with a pair of "pearl-handled colts" with other gang members Butch, Logan and Elzy Lay. 2.

Some people see a gun in this ghost picture, while others have commented to me they see a horse instead. It does look like the head of a mustang turned slightly downward and to the right toward the face, and you can see the horse is brown with a white nose. His right eye is shown, a full neck is there with a neck collar but no halter. There's even a small tuft of black mane hair atop his head. Those were the two things Sundance loved, guns and horses; not surprising they are superimposed on each other.

On the right of the large face is another horse, darker than the other one, his head held upright and also turned to the right. Look closely and you'll see incredible details: there is a rider with a square face upon this horse wearing a black bowler hat and a lighter shirt. His left arm is bent at the elbow, as though he were holding what is shaped like a rifle. If you compare this with the actual picture of the train car this horse and rider are not there. Maybe this is Bob Parker (Butch Cassidy).

Ghost pictures are always complex. For some, the longer you look at them the more you see. In this case there is a small face to the lower left, partially embedded into the dominant large face. This little face resembles Joe

LeFors, a member of the posse assembled after the Wilcox train robbery, below. He is seated far back on the left.

Joe LeFors

Joe LeFors was not a well-liked individual; the Pinkerton detective and bounty hunter Charles Siringo said LeFors was incompetent and that he despised him. LeFors was responsible for the hanging of Tom Horn and that accounted for his unpopularity, especially as many held the opinion that Horn was innocent and LeFors was an opportunist who fabricated the story that condemned him. LeFors got Horn to confess to the accidental shooting of a 14-year-old in a case of mistaken identity, but Horn was drunk and later said he was not fully cognizant of what he had said.

Adjacent to the main face, also connected to the upper left are a pair of large eyes with a sort of concerned expression. I have not been able to identify who this is; if you happen to find a match please write and let me know.

## Morphic Resonance

One way to understand how some of this works is to consider the morphic resonance hypothesis by Rupert Sheldrake in an astrophysical sense. The basic premise is energy cannot be destroyed and only changes form in the way it manifests. Therefore the memory of our lives exists in a consciousness field and persists after our bodies die. Little empirical evidence exists regarding this metaphysical science but here in this documentation seeing is believing so this phenomenon is actual.

Spirits often unite their energies together in a tour de force organization to be sure they manifest in photographs, and from my experience they often assume the same pose or near to that in the photographs taken when they were alive because that helps identify them. Applying this aspect to Sheldrake's theories this may be called the "influence of like upon like within a self-organized system," where people draw on a collective memory of their kind, sort of a tuning in that occurs electromagnetically.

This electromagnetic field theory is compatible with Newton's three laws of motion, the exception being the consolidation that space time IS the gravitational field and all dynamics are mediated through universal electromagnetic fields.

Here is the actual picture without the apparition(s):

This is one of the posses of rangers hired by the Union Pacific railroad in 1899 to go after Butch Cassidy's gang, led by Special Agent Timothy Keliher; not sure if Keliher is in this photo, but my guess is he is third from the left. LeFors does not appear to be in this picture; perhaps that lends to why he appears in the ghost photo.

Sheriff Jesse Tyler

Tragedy befell all the men killed by Kid Curry, alias Harvey Logan. Sheriff Jesse Tyler of the Grand County Sheriff's Department in Utah (above) was a particularly grievous loss since he was 43, single and had been an orphan as his parents died when he was a young boy. His grandparents came from London to Beaver County in 1833, but it was assumed they and their children had all been killed by Indians. Jesse was born in 1857.

Sheriff Tyler was shot in the back by Harvey Logan, aka Kid Curry on May 26, 1900, while approaching a camp on Hill Creek, Utah in a search for outlaws. 3. This location is forty-three miles north of Thompson Springs in the Book Mountains. The other officer killed was Deputy Samuel F. Jenkins, also shot in the back by Logan. A third lawman, Deputy Herman Day escaped. Deputy Day was fifty yards from the shootings but could not get over to assist. As soon as Tyler and Jenkins were killed Day started for help. The outlaws shot at him twice but missed him.

An article written in the Grand Valley Times says Sheriff Tyler was a "man of sterling integrity" and known by many friends as "Honest Jack." The fearlessness Tyler knew when doing his job "bordered at times onto carelessness of his own life." 4. When Tyler and Jenkins discovered the camp they thought it was Indians, and so left their rifles on their saddles. The last words Sheriff Tyler spoke were "Hello Boys" before they were gunned down. The detailed story of the killings is found under the heading "Killed by Outlaws" of the same paper above, same date as referenced.

Another completely different account of this shootout says it was a planned revenge killing by Logan that happened in Moab, Utah against Sheriff Tyler and Deputy Jenkins because they killed Logan's good friend George

Curry and George's brother Lonny. Tyler is well regarded; just go to odmp.org/officer/13524-sheriff-jesse-tyler to see the many thoughtful messages left for him.

A bittersweet ending to the story of Sheriff Tyler took place in 1995, when a relative from London named John Tyler recognized him in a picture as a family member because his looks were identical to that of John's father and uncle. John Tyler corroborated that some of his family members had moved to Beaver County, Utah in 1833.

## Personal Facts of the Sundance Kid

Harry Alonzo Longabaugh whose surname is Old German for "ready for battle" & "noble" was born in 1867 in Mont Clare, near Pennsylvania which is in the lower right corner of the state. Longabaugh is pronounced "Long- a- bau" as in bending the waist in a respectful gesture, or the front part of a ship.

He was no slouch; his posture and appearance reflects the genteel meaning of his name. Quickness on the draw was his readiness and what kept him from having to kill other men: he always got the draw on them and they backed down. The particulars of his features are found on this card below from South America describing him: bright blue azure eyes and chestnut hair with a reddish tint to it. It also says his overall facial look resembles a "Greek" type and that he has a rather long nose. The long nose comment is an interesting one and merits a reference to the Hebrew "erech apaim" which means when God has a long nose He is slow to anger; conversely, when a nose is scrunched up it shows anger. I believe this also reflects the personality of Sundance, that he was an even-tempered individual not prone to anger.

**..OS RETRATOS, SEÑAS PERSONALES Y LA HISTORIA CRIMINAL DE CADA UNO DE LOS INDIVIDUOS SOSPECHOSOS, SE DAN Á CONTINUACIÓN.**

HARRY LONGBAUGH

The card above is a translated partial excerpt taken from a Pinkerton National Detective Agency notice on three outlaws: Butch, Sundance and a deaf man named Camilla Hanks. The actual photo of Harry used in the Pinkerton paper was taken on November 21, 1900, when he was 33 years old and was taken from the famous photo "The Fort Worth Five," when the gang posed in Fort Worth, Texas: this included Sundance, Ben Kilpatrick, Cassidy (seated) Will Carver and Harvey Logan (standing).

The Pinkerton National Detective Agency was the FBI of the time. They held their main office in Chicago and had been hired to hunt down the James gang in 1874, then later during the era of westward frontier expansion hunted after Butch Cassidy's gang. By the 1890's they were 2,000 detectives and 30,000 reserve officers strong.

Public sentiment was not in favor of the Pinkerton agency, particularly after the botched raid on the Jesse James home in Missouri in 1875 when they blew up the house, resulting in the death of Jesse's 9-year-old half-brother. The explosion partially blew off his mother Zerelda Samuel's arm, and the James brothers were not even there. Decades later Pinkertons were hired as security guards for big business industries and to quell against union strikes. In an 1882 strike a dozen iron and steel workers were actually killed in the clash, and this made the Pinkertons extremely unpopular. Today the Pinkertons are a private security firm and still operate under the name "Pinkerton."

## A Brief Chronological Sample of His Life

When Harry Longabaugh was 15 in 1882 he and his cousin George, George's wife Mary Yantis and infant Walter traveled from Shelby County, Illinois to Durango, Colorado by covered wagon. George was from Harry's great grand-uncle Balser's side of the family. There is no record for a "George" that I could find; perhaps he was a distant cousin of Harry's. Having said that it makes sense that local oral tradition in the Durango area claims that George was already there and Harry Longabaugh came with someone else to meet up with him, but there is no information on who that someone else was. Cousin George and his wife were the same people at the Colorado location that gave Harry sanctuary from the law in later years when he became the Sundance Kid and took part in the robbing of a Telluride bank in 1899.

George wanted to homestead in Colorado, but Harry left in 1886 (age 19) and went to Montana. A year later while in Sundance, Montana, Harry stole a horse and a gun from a cowboy, earning the nickname "The Sundance Kid." He was arrested in 1887 near the Three V Ranch in Miles City, Montana and sentenced to 18 months in jail. For a while after he got out of jail he bounced around between Canada and Montana rustling cattle and horses. He was skilled at rounding up wild range horses, breaking and selling them, having learned horse breeding and such while working at various ranches. He was a seasoned rustler, a hold up criminal and generally a tough character throughout his younger years.

Nine years later when he was 29 in 1896 he met Robert Leroy Parker, alias Butch Cassidy as Cassidy was getting out of jail. Their notorious alliance included numerous bank, saloon and train robberies, one of the most notable being the holdup of the Union Pacific Overland Flyer #1 train on June 2, 1899, in Wilcox, Wyoming at 1am in the morning. It was reported that there were two shootouts en route while escaping to the hideout: the first 10 miles from Casper and the second 30 miles from Casper; the former is where Sheriff Hazen was shot in the stomach- he died later in Douglas. Several horses were also killed in the shootouts. According to Tom Horn 5. who worked on and off for the Pinkertons, the gang members were in Medicine Bow, which is just a few miles west of Wilcox the night before the hold up when Elzy Lay rode in to tell them what the train would be carrying.

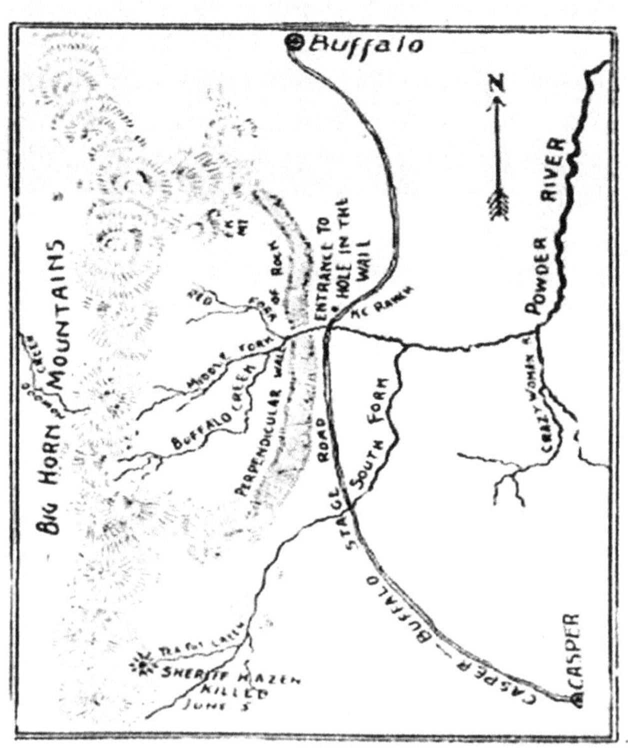

After the first day of the chase the robbers split up and three got away. The Globe newspaper of South Bethlehem, Pennsylvania on June 7, 1899, reported the three remaining robbers retreated to a "natural fort among the rocks" where they were penned in by the posse. 6. However the robbers escaped under the cover of night. The article ends by saying the robbers were heading for the Hole in the Wall. It was noted through several newspaper sources that they stole between $34,000 and $50,000 and some bank notes. This was a very carefully planned out robbery by Butch Cassidy who was a mastermind at meticulous detail and deception to boot. He had two of his men William Pierce and Edward Agar board the train with carpet bags full of lead shots. This explains why the car, pictured below was shredded to smithereens, because the lead shot must have been used by mixing it in with dynamite.

To start, one or two of Butch's men flagged down the train with warning lanterns. The location was precise, as the Hole in the Wall gang stopped the train just before it would have crossed the bridge, separated the locomotive and mail cars from the passengers, then had the front cars cross the bridge, leaving all the passengers on the other side of the bridge. Then they dynamited the bridge. Cassidy and Sundance even had a backup plan to secure fresh horses if needed from a few friendly ranchers they knew. It is likely Butch and Sundance split up, each leading a group of three in separate directions. The three robbers running from the posse the longest headed north from Wilcox into the Big Horn Mountains towards the Hole in the Wall hideout in a likely rendezvous with the others that escaped earlier. The posse had been on their trail but lost them in the Big Horns. Butch had a trick he learned from Indians, and that was putting moccasins on horses' hoofs so they would not leave tracks.

Pertaining to Sundance in this particular heist he was likely operating under the name of Harry Alonzo, a different alias from one he sported in South Dakota in 1897 when he robbed a bank under the name Frank Jones. This may be why in Tom Horn's account of the three bandits who were running together one was called "a Mexican." Butch may have donned the alias Jim Lowe, a name he had used in robberies in 1898. The identities of the train robbery outlaws were a mystery for a while but were eventually traced to the Hole in the Wall gang. Pinkerton identified participants in the holdup as Cassidy, Sundance, Elzy Lay, William Pierce, Edward Agar and Harvey Logan.

The original location of the Hole in the Wall Cabin was upwards of a remote and secluded pass called the Hole in the Wall Pass south of the foothills of the Big Horn Mountains in Johnson County, Wyoming. It was built on Buffalo Creek west of Kaycee, Wyoming in 1883 by Alexander Ghent who records show died in 1884. The Hole in the Wall is located due west about mid-way between

Buffalo and Casper. At one time there were six cabins there where many outlaws spent harsh winters; they were untouchable there, for it was very difficult for lawmen to get to because the one-horse trail up was narrow and the outlaws could see them coming for miles around. There is also a cave close by where the cabin ranch house was.

There were so many robberies that Harry Longabaugh participated in during his career that it is not my intention to write about all of them. That would take me a year and is not the purpose of this. I am trying to reveal the true, objectionable nature of the man by offering details as he might have wanted. When he was in the Custer County jail in Miles City back in June 8, 1887 he gave a statement to the Yellowstone Journal that he wanted the truth about his intentions to be known:

*"I read a very sensational and partly untrue article, which places me before the public not even second to the notorious Jesse James. Admitting that I have done wrong and expecting to be dealt with according to law and not by false reports from parties who should blush with shame to make them, I ask a little of your space to set my case before the public in a true light. In the first place I have always worked for an honest living; was employed last summer by one of the best ranches…"* -Harry Alonzo Longabaugh 1887

When one is sitting in jail there is a lot of time to think. These statements sound like someone who wants to be seen for what he is. What he is saying is he's not as bad as folks make him out to be and he is not a violent person, and that he is honest and wants truthful reports about him- not sensational inaccurate opinions. Even back then fake news was a problem. After all, although known as the best shot of the gang he never killed anyone.

Of course, he was only 19 at the time Longabaugh said this quote and his notorious career was still at its early stages as he continued breaking the law after he joined up with Robert Leroy Parker.

"All things are permitted for me, but I will not be mastered by anything." (1 Corinthians 6:12) In this passage we see not only self-control, but the awareness that one can do wrongful things if so choosing but does not because of Christ. This would apply to Harry's moral conscience when he avoided killing whenever he shot at someone. However, Sundance did deliberately choose the path of crime and therefore was in charge of his own destiny. His cognitive dissonance then may be why he is still appearing today. Perhaps he wants us to pray for his soul, or at least to understand what he felt when he was alive.

In the interest of gaining an accurate contextual perspective into the outlaw mind, it is helpful to look at the culture of the time and why people were behaving the way they were. My point is it wouldn't be completely fair to judge another time period's different historical operations by today's standards. Guerilla warfare during the Civil War persisted post-war, especially in Kansas and Missouri; the latter state was where Jesse James (1847-1882) was from. There were numerous fights over settlement rights resulting in a breakdown of lawful society, corruption was widespread, and it was not uncommon for people to take the law into their own hands. It was typical for a killer to become a deputy or sheriff or even a judge, and thus decide the case in his favor. Ironically, a criminal turned lawman could be known as noble hearted and assertive. This was the case with Wyatt Earp (1848-1949), who was initially arrested in 1871 in Van Buren, Arkansas for horse theft. By the time the gunfight at the O.K. Corral took place in 1873 he had been deputized by his brother Virgil, who was the Marshall of Tombstone, a one-time silver mining town. Newspapers were widespread and tended to portray such men as almost heroic. It was this tone of public approval that helped set the precedent for the rise of crime that moved westward and produced wild west outlaws such as Cassidy and Sundance.

The south had become devastated during and after the Civil War, and so most outlaws at this time were Democratic Confederate sympathizers, and there was widespread negative sentiment toward greedy "Yankee capitalist banks." Around 1870 larger banks became harder to rob because time locks were installed, so outlaws turned to robbing trains.

When the actions of certain lawmen became unbearable vigilante justice took over, such as in the case of Sheriff Clark of Telluride, who was shot in the back dead in August of 1895 on Main Street in Telluride. At that time Telluride was a rough mining town. Someone killed him because Clark had been suspiciously and conveniently absent when Butch Cassidy robbed the San Miguel County bank in Telluride on June 24, 1889 with two other men. They stole twenty thousand dollars, comparatively equivalent to half a million today. According to one source Cyrus "Doc" Shores said Clark was paid $2200 for his cooperation. Incidentally, it has been noted that when the robbers got a handful of miles away the Sundance Kid awaited with fresh horses to continue their escape into the Mancos Mountains.

The picture below is of telluride in the 1880's:

Each individual alone is responsible for the choices he makes. God does not condone sin but there is a difference between sin done out of weakness or ignorance that assumes the sin is acceptable, and those sins done when you know it's wrong. Once sin is manifest in the heart as a way of life the conscience is gone and repentance is no longer possible. You only have time to repent from sin while alive, but you are out of time after you die. Let's hope that Harry Longabaugh had faith and believed somehow his sins were forgivable.

*"Labour to keep alive in your breast that little celestial fire called conscience."* 7.

George Washington recommended this, and he's trying to help us keep in touch with God through our moral character. In the complex society of today this can be difficult due to too much stimulation and demands put upon you. If you sit quietly and listen your heart will reveal to you what to do or not to do. The anxiety of the mind can confuse, but never the heart, for it knows the truth by instinct. A conflict between the two can be when you find yourself in the middle of a situation where you feel a certain tinge of guilt; again, this is cognitive dissonance. If you keep feeling it then your heart is telling you to get out of that situation. You will feel better after you do that. However, guilt is relative to the conditions in which you live, as in the case of the Sundance Kid, where the absence of it is explained pertaining to the time frame he lived within. In a general sense we are products of our environment, so we can't easily judge people who lived long ago by today's standards- that would be dismissing the context in which these occurrences happened and would be unfair to not consider variables of that.

In some situations two people cannot get along because they cannot agree on what truth is. What is relevant to someone may not matter to another. For example, citizens often viewed outlaws like Butch Cassidy and the Sundance Kid as heroes when they came to a small town and gave away money. It wasn't until they robbed a bank that held money to pay miners that public favoritism towards them began to fade, and the Pinkertons were employed to hunt them down.

## A Note on Butch Cassidy

Robert Leroy Parker, alias Butch Cassidy (April 13, 1866-1937, 71 years) in particular hated authority figures, a development that began when his father Maximillian Parker lost a land dispute in Circleville, Utah. The Parkers were Mormons but not active church goers.

Bored on the farm, he wrote his mother in 1884 when he was 18:

*"Ma, there's not much here for me. No future. Pay in Utah is low – you know that. Maybe twenty or thirty dollars a month with board – and the board's not much to brag about in most places. There's no excitement around here. I'm not a kid anymore. Gotta be thinking about my future."* 8.

After Robert worked on a cattle and horse farm for a nearby cowboy named Mike Cassidy he took on the name and became Butch Cassidy. The "Butch" part came from when he worked for a short while as a butcher. He was a brilliant criminal and could constantly outthink his would-be captors.

## Debunking the Myths

So much speculation has evolved around the Sundance Kid's life and those around him. One such contrivance was his supposed marriage to Luzernia Morrell of Duchesne, Utah in 1894. Some fictional finders purported Harry had taken over the identity of William Henry Long while marrying his widow who had six children. First of all she was 36 years old in 1894 and Longabaugh was 27, an unlikely match. The real Bill Long died in 1936 and is buried in Duchesne City Cemetery, Utah. When he was exhumed in 2009 a bullet hole was found in his skull, so that set in motion an investigation on his death. It was discovered that at the time of Long's death a rifle had been found next to the body and his death had been ruled as a suicide. However it's really hard to shoot yourself in the head with a rifle, so the 2009 investigators suspected it might be a murder. Besides, forensics revealed there were no traces of powder burns on his hands and the angle of entry of the bullet showed it was not possible to have killed himself. So it remains a mystery of who killed Bill Long? We may never know, but the following year after his death Luzernia died and is in the plot next to her husband. Somehow the Sundance Kid doesn't fit into this picture. Furthermore, the DNA test on Bill Long does not match any descendant family members of Harry Longabaugh. Case closed on that one.

Then there is the claim Robert Harvey Longabaugh (2-21-1901 to 12-18-1972) made that he was the son of the Sundance Kid. Harry Longabaugh was not in Oregon at the time (1900) Robert claims Sundance had an affair with his mother. There has been no evidence to support any part of his story and he changed his accounts several times. Moreover, the Pinkerton Detectives said they have found nothing indicating Sundance had affairs with any women other than Etta Place after 1899.

Rumors were out that Harry Longabaugh's family had relocated to Atlantic City, New Jersey in 1902, and that he and Etta Place had visited them there in 1902. However there are no apparent property records there of his immediate family, and most of them including his mother, father, and two sisters are buried at Morris Cemetery in Phoenixville, Chester County, Pennsylvania, near in physical proximity to where they were originally from. I don't know why several family members would move 200 miles then be buried back where they came from; sounds improbable. His brother Harvey Sylvester Longabaugh is also buried in Pennsylvania. If any Longabaughs were in New Jersey Harry and Etta did not stay with them, for there are records that show they checked in at Mrs. Thompson's Boarding House on April 2, 1902, then toured Coney Island. You have to remember that these were people in hiding and constantly on the run, so to obfuscate any data on themselves would be to their advantage.

The three of them Butch, Harry and Etta went to Buenos Aires, Argentina after Butch, Sundance and Harvey Logan, alias Kid Curry robbed a train called the Great Northern Express near Wagner, Montana on a Wednesday afternoon on July 3, 1901 where they stole between $40,000 to $60,000. It was their last train robbery. They left New York City for South America on Feb. 20, 1902; the year is not documented but their departure had to have been after the robbery. They returned on March 3, 1902. Four months later on July 10, 1902 Harry and Etta boarded the steamer Honorius and went back to Argentina.

The three of them made several trips back and forth from the U.S. to South America and were well versed on how to travel those itineraries. Robert Parker was more elusive and careful to conceal himself and is not cited (pun intended) as much during his travels as Longabaugh and Place.

*"A plan in the heart of a person is like deep water, but a person of understanding draws it out."* (Proverbs 20:5 NAS) If you list the sequence of facts available, a coherent picture develops that fills in the evident gaps. They were always extremely careful and paid attention to details.

## Etta Place

There were rumors that Butch Cassidy found Etta in a cathouse in Texas in 1892 that have never been substantiated. Robert Parker and Harry Longabaugh were masters at disguising who they were and every tittle of identity that could be twisted was done to thwart their capture. Someone told a Pinkerton detective Etta was from Texas and that was documented by them in 1902 [9]. but there is no evidence that she was.

Facts about Etta may have been confused with the life of Annie Porter 1873-1940 (67 yrs), a Proprietor who ran a very successful brothel on 503 South San Saba Street in San Antonio. Annie Porter was often the girlfriend of Harvey "Kid Curry" Logan, who was well known as a womanizer. They had met at Fannie's Boarding House.

The only documented visit to Texas that involved Etta Place was in the summer of 1904 when she and Harry visited the Saint Louis World Fair then went on to Forth Worth, Texas. It is noted that she mistakenly signed her name on a hotel register as "Ethel" and that is why people assumed Ethel was her real name. However, back to the case in point that the game was all about disguise to keep the law guessing.

In early 1905 the three of them sold their ranch in Argentina, narrowly escaping Pinkerton officers. The story is Sheriff Edward Humphreys tipped them off because he had a crush on Etta, so they escaped by sailing to Chile on May 1, 1905. This is an example of why it was invaluable to have a woman included in the entourage; it was probably conveyed that she was a relative but not a wife. Here Harry Longabaugh uses the same trick Abraham used with his wife Sarah in Genesis 20:2, when they were in a foreign land and he tells her to pretend she is his sister for protection of his life. Incidentally, Sarah really was Abraham's half-sister: they had the same father but a different mother. People had no knowledge of DNA before the twentieth century and did not realize the detriments of having children with a relative.

Etta wanted to come home, so on June 30, 1906 Harry dropped her off in San Francisco. Records of her living there persist through 1907 then she mysteriously disappears. It is an odd coincidence that Harry's brother Elwood Place Longabaugh was originally buried at Laurel Hill Cemetery, San Francisco in 1930, but when the city confiscated the land 35 thousand bodies were relocated to other cemeteries. Elwood was moved to Cypress Memorial Park in Colma, San Mateo County, California between 1937 and 1941. Elwood's grave is marked, but there are "Unknown" graves at the Cypress cemetery as well. Apparently all older cemeteries have graves marked "Unknown." The question remains what Elwood was doing in San Francisco 2000 miles away from home in Pennsylvania, and if it is really Elwood that is buried there.

Although she was in San Francisco in 1907 she returned to Antofagasta, Chile in 1909, where she asked the U.S. Vice Counsul Frank Aller for a death certificate for Harry Longabaugh. Aller would not issue it. Etta tried again to obtain a death certificate on July 3, 1909 in Bolivia, claiming she needed to settle his estate.

No one likes to be alone and given the nature of most people one can assume Etta went back home at some point. While she had lived a short while in Chile, residents there who knew her said she told them she was from the east coast of the United States. She may have been one of Harry's many cousins, which explains why she used the surname Place. It is possible Sundance was in love with his cousin, not unusual for the time. As mentioned earlier it is likely that he and Butch had decided it would be a good cover to travel with a lady, so at first glance no one would think they were outlaws. She may have been Emma J. Longabaugh 1860-1944 (84 yrs), the daughter of Harry's uncle Michael Longabaugh 1825-1908 (82 yrs). Both Michael and Emma are buried at Morris Cemetery.

## Professional Photo

While visiting their family in Mont Clare, Pennsylvania in 1901 Harry and Etta had stopped along the way to get their picture taken in New York City on Broadway. This is the best known photo of Etta with Harry taken in February of 1901 by the Bliss Brothers studio, whose business address was 368 Main Street, Buffalo, New York. The cover picture for this documentation is taken from this same photo, and this is where Harry's face matches the face in the ghost picture the best, especially the dominant right eye and longer nose.

Obviously your soul doesn't die. The Sundance Kid broke the commandment law "Thou shalt not steal" more than any other commandment and the price he paid was being forced to run and hide in obscurity; definitely not a normal existence. He died in obscurity as well because we don't know where he is buried. For that we can only speculate. His ghost showed up with his horse at his old hideaway cabin, still brandishing his gun. Perhaps he would like us to pray for him so he may be forgiven and go to a better place than being earth bound. Prayers are powerful and God does hear them.

*"A prayer of a righteous person, when it is brought about, can accomplish much."* -James 5:16

We cannot romanticize the life of outlaws because much of their lives were a series of wrongful actions, albeit some felt the constant guilt from doing so. Since judgement is God's strange work we can only pray for the soul that wants to be forgiven. Perhaps Harry had faith when alive in the flesh, although his works present a problem. As I said earlier ghosts show up for a reason, and I believe he wants help for his soul. In Luke 16:19-31 even the man in hell can still think, feel and has the ability to remember and reason.

Then there is the criminal who was crucified alongside Christ. In a final declaration of faith he states to the other criminal "we are receiving what we deserve for our crimes, but this man has done nothing wrong...Jesus, remember me when You come into Your kingdom!" (Luke 23:41-42 NAS) Jesus replied "you will be with me in paradise" (Luke 23:43 NAS) One can only hope it is not too late for Harry Longabaugh to seek mercy.

## They Faked Their Own Deaths

Butch and Sundance were not at the Bolivian shootout on November 7, 1908 for several reasons:

-They were perfectly acquainted with boarding ships to and from South American departure ports, travel lines and destinations. If a problem arose at a location where they were, as seasoned escape artists they would have slipped away.

-There were several American bandits also hiding in South America that they knew and would likely have interfaced with while abroad or at South American locations. Butch could have put together a well thought out set-up to have other outlaws who resembled them killed to fake their deaths. With a long-range plan in mind, he probably invited some outlaw friends to South America earlier, during all the back and forth trips he and Harry took.

-The stolen branded mule that was placed conspicuously in front of the American outlaws rented house in San Vicente, Bolivia drew the Bolivian police there. Butch and Sundance would have never been so careless.

-The 1991 DNA tests done on the exhumed American outlaws killed in the Bolivian shootout do not match any Parker or Longabaugh relatives. The tests were done by forensic anthropologist Clyde Snow.

- Butch's sister Lula Parker Betenson said Butch returned to the family ranch in Circleville, Utah in 1925,

Lula Betenson

and at that time he visited his father and attended a wedding. Butch's father died in 1938 and is at the Circleville Cemetery, and his mother passed away decades before in 1905; also buried at the Circleville Cemetery. Lula added her brother lived out his life in the state of Washington, died in 1937 and is buried in an unmarked grave at the Parowan Cemetery in Utah which is 18 miles from Circleville.

Another account by Fred Adams, son of Paul Adams the pastor who presided over Butch's niece's funeral thinks Butch Cassidy is in grave #20 next to his brother Dan Parker. Paul Adams said Butch had made an appearance at his niece's gravesite at the Parowan Cemetery where he paid Paul Adams in large bills for her burial expenses. It seems to me his sister's account would be the more credible of the two regarding where he is buried. Moreover, Butch's nephew Bill Betenson said his great-grandmother Lula had the clear details of the location of Butch's burial which was a family secret and would remain that way.

Something that doesn't add up are the details on the life of a S.G. Longabaugh 1866-1915 (49 yrs), who sometimes appears on searches as Harry Alonzo Longabaugh's brother, and other times does not. S.G. Longabaugh is not buried where most of the family is; instead he is at the Saint Louis Cemetery in Kentucky. There is nothing that tells us what the "S.G." stands for, and no information on where he was born either. Annie G. Place who was Sundance's mother is buried at Morris Cemetery, and searches on her do not bring up S.G. as her son. Maybe Sundance is buried in S. G.'s grave and S.G. stands for "Sundance's Grave." Just a thought.

1. *The Beyond is Part of the Here Now Book 2. © 2020 June Raleigh. All rights reserved. Available on Amazon & Ingram.*
2. *The Wild Bunch Chronicles. A Timeline From 1890-1910 © Vince Garcia. All rights reserved..*
3. *True West Magazine. Mark Boardman. Let Sleeping Outlaws Lie. Sheriff Jesse Tyler Awoke the Wrong Men. July 27, 2020. © 2021 True West Magazine*
4. *Utah Digital Newspapers. Grand Valley Times. 1900-06-01. Sheriff Jesse Tyler*
5. *Tom Horn: Blood on the Moon by Chip Carlson. High Plains Press, 1st edition. Available on Amazon.*
6. *The Globe. South Bethlehem, Pennsylvania. June 7, 1899. Battles with Robbers. Item #562759*
7. *Washington, George, Rules of Civility, 110th rule, © 1988 by Applewood Books.*
8. *Hadley Meares. Biography magazine. Butch Cassidy and the Sundance Kid: The True Story of the Famous Outlaws. Aug. 22, 2019. Updated Sept. 8, 2020*
9. *Pinkerton National Detective Agency. Library of Congress, Washington, D.C. 2001*

# Requiem for the Ghost of the Sundance Kid

As this book is a non-fictional work it can be regarded as epistemological evidence: the method employed is to provide you with true accounts, complimented with biblical passages. You can then decide the validity of the contents for yourself. Included in the first chapter is an actual picture of an apparition, and since seeing is believing documentation of this sighting separates fact from opinion, proving there is life after death. That is the main intention of this writing, that you the reader realize your soul lives on after your body dies.

"Cogito, ergo sum" 1. Descartes said this, and it translates to "I think, therefore I am." Descartes later changes it a bit to say "I am, I exist" in his Meditations on First Philosophy. It is a metaphysical realization to know you are here because you are reading this right now.

What Descartes said is close to what God replies to Moses in Exodus 3:14 when he describes Himself "I am who I am" (New American Standard). Jesus echoes this in John 8:58 "Truly, truly I say to you, before Abraham came into being, I am" (NAS). This is affirmation that any living entity knows it is alive.

The soul exists outside its former body and it is sometimes still visible in the material realm. That is basically what we here today are leaning toward; that is, pondering the afterlife. There is an obvious difference between the waking and sleeping states; the fact that the ghost appears to us in our waking state makes it a point of interest to ask how he does so, and how conscious he is, for he certainly exists, as Descartes proves in his modified statement.

In the case of Sundance there is no defined duality that we can see of awake or asleep attributed to him; clearly his ghost is just there and we see him. For example, we are locked into a cycle of sleep, then we awaken, but when we die is it possible we actually go into a permanent state of being awake? We cannot know what state the ghost is in, we can only assume he is awake, because we are awake.

*1. René Descartes, Discourse on the Method, 1637*

# CHAPTER 2
# The Gym Teacher

When you grow up in Los Angeles you fully experience a diverse plethora of cultures, or as some say "a melting pot." At Richard Garvey Intermediate High School (now called a middle school) there were large Latino gangs that lived in the areas around the school. Conspicuous during snack and lunch times, they roamed about the campus in groups of half a dozen or so. An eighth-grade female gang was led by a certain girl they called "Weta" which is slang for "white girl" in Spanish. In this case it was not meant in a derogatory way but rather as a compliment, as the leader of this girl gang herself insisted that was what everyone was to call her. She must have spent an hour or more every morning applying make-up, for when you looked at her face there were several layers of foundation, thick eyeliner, powders and eyeshadow colors reminiscent of a rainbow.

One day during lunch while meandering around the building walkway Elaine and Julie were caught staring at her, fascinated by Weta's make up. Turning to face them she asked menacingly "what you looking at gringa?" Elaine recoiled saying "nothing" and moved away, for no one wanted to be jumped and beat up by this aggressive group of young girls. Everyone saw them coming and avoided their path, but some unlucky gals got pushed around and had their purses taken away from them. After one of these sad events happened to their friend Laurie, Elaine and Julie stopped carrying purses to avoid victimization. Besides, who needs a purse when you are fourteen years old; back pockets are sufficient for stashing your money. Most girls didn't wear makeup yet so it wasn't a priority to carry lipstick and such.

When you're in the eighth grade it's all about looking for love, and you can be picky then because the first time for love is special. It's a confusing time too because going through puberty is awkward and you're feeling this all-powerful drive to find a boyfriend, or girlfriend if you're a male. Trying to understand what's happening is challenging to say the least. Then there's approval from peers, the single most important variable for that age group, but trying to have an active social life while keeping up grades is hard, so most teens just focus on getting good grades during the week while trying to set up social interactions on weekends.

One Friday in gym class in early June, Elaine and Julie were playing softball out on the field, Julie hitting a single to first base and generally enjoying the fourth period class that day. As usual the bell rings at the end of class then they all walk to the girl's gym building, go to the locker areas and pile into the required showers before getting dressed again. Elaine had just finished dressing when she heard a commotion at the far end of the showers adjacent to the front door of the gym. She slammed her locker shut and walked briskly over to the shower stalls to see what was happening. Yep, Weta and her gang were at it again, this time in protest over showering against the orders of the gym teacher Ms. Ramey. Four members including the leader of the gang stood together at the entrance of the stall but out of the reach of the shower spray, still fully dressed while Ms. Ramey was reprimanding them for not participating in gym class activities. The gang gals were shouting they didn't need to shower since they had not exercised. The teacher was trying to explain to them why they were going to fail her class, her finger pointing repeatedly at her clipboard. The girls grew angry and did not like hearing this.

Ms. Ramey had on navy shorts and a white collared short sleeve shirt, as was the uniform for all gym teachers and students, and stood armed with her chart referring to what she wrote in it at the girls, warning and insisting they were failing gym. Weta and her friends had become so self-absorbed into asserting their gang power and rebellion against the system they argued aggressively and defiantly with the gym teacher to her face. Frustrated and angry, Ms. Ramey pointed her finger in the gang leader's face when Elaine saw Weta suddenly push the teacher back with enough force that she slipped and fell backwards into the shower stall, her head slamming down hard onto the tile. Elaine stared in disbelief stunned at what she was witnessing, for never had she imagined that a student would lay hands on a teacher with violent force. Ms. Ramey clutched at her chest and with an agonized expression on her face stopped moving.

Time slowed down in those awful moments, her mind registering a permanent surreal snapshot of Ms. Ramey lying there with the shower water sprinkling onto her lifeless body, still clutching her chart which now sat upon her right chest area, water permeating everything. While she stared voices around her became dull and incomprehensible. The Latina gang ran past her darting out the front doors all at once. Several girls were now coming onto the scene asking what happened, when

Laurie exclaimed "they killed Ms. Ramey!" There was screaming and running for help, but Elaine stood in shock not knowing what to do at this time, watching the only movement she could see which was the glistening shower water beating down on her teacher's lifeless body, with beams of light streaming from the high windows above that reached her lying there. Immediately the other two gym teachers emerged from their offices in the back of the building and ushered the crowd back, telling the girls to go to lunch while several staff came quickly to help. Alas, the teacher had expired on that wet tile in the last few weeks of the school year.

*"The rod and reproof give wisdom; But a child left to himself causeth shame to his mother.* -Proverbs 29:15 (NAS)

These girls who rebelled against order and refused to be disciplined killed their teacher. If the gang leader had parents that had taught her violence was wrong she most likely would not have been a violent person at such a young age, or ever. It is anyone's guess how the parents of these girls reacted when they learned of the incident, or if they were even told. A school can only do so much with children. Teachers take them as they arrive into the classrooms, ready or not to learn. How terrible it is when thoughtless children take away energy from the learning capacity in a school and cause the whole system to suffer. Above all, that hard-working gym teacher didn't deserve to die like that.

Elaine and Julie have plenty of Hispanic friends that are friendly and focused on academics. This account is not to say in any way that all Latinos are gang members. When they are though, they can be very formidable, as this group was. There are good and bad in every race and many factors that determine how a child behaves in society.

Everyone talked about the death of Ms. Ramey until school quickly ended in June. Closure was followed by a lazy summer that year. Late in July Elaine and Julie went to see a little league baseball game out on the field adjacent to their former gym. They had a fun time, feeling like superior graduates yet nostalgically cheering on the school team, for they were not to return there after that day. Instead, they would be in the freshmen class attending Mark Keppel High School in Alhambra next month.

Everyone left the field area when the game ended, but Elaine and Julie remained on the right side of the second row near the bottom bench of the bleachers, reminiscing about how life had been at Garvey Intermediate. Julie said "I really liked my Science teacher Mr. Philip- he got me interested in being a lab technician someday." Elaine said her elective class in sewing was so much fun that maybe she would be a clothes designer in the future. For both teens the prospects of high school were very exciting to look forward to.

A figure approaching from the left caught Elaine's eye and she turned to see who was still on the field, having thought they were alone. Ten feet in front of them Ms. Ramey strode by, holding her clip board and smiling at them as she said "Hi girls!" Ms. Ramey looked like she was dressed for the job in the usual navy shorts and white shirt, looking exactly as they had last seen her. In fact she looked more energetic than ever and beamed with light. "Hi" answered a dumbfounded Elaine, reacting without thinking, without remembering that this lady had died right in front of her a few weeks ago. The teacher turned the corner around the bleachers. Elaine looked at Julie for support but Julie's jaw had dropped and no words were coming out. They both turned to the right to see where their gym teacher was going but Ms. Ramey had vanished. Elaine stood up and jumped down to the ground, turning quickly around, searching for the lady but she was nowhere to be found. Checking the gate behind them they saw the small opening had not been accessed and was still closed. If it had been opened they would have heard the squeaky hinges move as when they had previously entered from there. "Wasn't that Ms. Ramey? Where'd she go?" asked Julie. "She died- how could that be her?" said Elaine.

The hair on the back of their necks stood up, full of dread because something had happened that their fifteen and a half years could not explain. They left quickly, got into the Volkswagen that Elaine had borrowed from her mom and drove to Elaine's house. Once in her room they spoke quietly about what they had seen. "You know she looked happy" remarked Julie. They had a long conversation about death, God and the soul. Neither one ever returned to their old school again.

One cannot accurately summarize that Ms. Ramey's energy was a residual haunting because residual hauntings do not interact with the viewer. Her ghost clearly interacted with the two teens when she acknowledged them and even spoke "Hi girls!" This shows the ghost was present during real time. Elaine had been at the scene when Ms. Ramey passed away; perhaps this lent strength to and triggered some kind of empathetic connection and memory that otherwise wouldn't have been there.

The gym teacher's death had not been a natural one; instead it had been forced on her with a degree of violence, and so perhaps her soul remains and wants closure so she can leave. One of Elaine's friends Laurie had witnessed the event of Ms. Ramey's death and had given an eye witness account to law enforcement.

Ms. Ramey's energy may still walk the campus. We can only wish her well and pray she has gone to a better place.

## Choices and Consequences

Motivations cause actions, and our free will exercises those choices. Almost everything we do, and even some things we don't choose to do have a motivation behind it. When we donate to charity we are hoping to help the world better itself. We deliberately take actions that carry out our choices.

Contrarily, one may not wish to sleep but when he does he is rejuvenating mind and body and wakes up refreshed; eventually he is forced to give in. This is the difference between motivational actions that are deliberate and those that are automatic. In the cases where there is no choice or free will you are functioning in a design or pattern where fate takes over, such as when your body needs sleep, or food to eat. No choice there, you just do it.

We humans love freedom and like to break out of patterns if we can. It's just our stubborn nature, but some things you cannot change. If rebelliousness is carried out too far a person can become stubborn to a fault.

The actions of the rebellious teens at the middle school led to the consequences where their gym teacher died. In essence they killed her: not pre-meditatively, but they did directly cause her death. What's astounding is no penalties or repercussions were imposed on the guilty party due to the fact that they were minors, which may be the cause of why Ms. Ramey cannot rest.

When tragedy befalls society such as a mass shooting of innocent people the public always expresses sadness and looks to preventative measures. In the case of murder there can be no deterrent prevention except the awaiting penalty. The solution is in the effective outcome or penalty for the crime. The criminal who knows they will not die as a result of killing fearlessly goes right on ahead and takes away the lives of others. The most that can happen, and he knows this is he will get life imprisonment, something that is somewhat appealing to him, since that means he will get a warm jail cell with three meals a day.

In countries where historically the murderer by law was buried alive with the corpse of the person they killed or executed outright, there was and still is very little crime. In these places that follow biblical law when a person stole their hand was cut off, and you can be sure very few persons killed or stole. A friend of mine from Egypt told me these were the laws of his country, and although crime exists today it is not a real problem. Today Egypt executes by hanging, not the ghastly live burial as before. They do not always publish their capital punishment statistics, but between August 2020 and August 2021 there were 176 executions out of a population of 102 million people. This is a small number (0.0000172%), approximately 1.73 persons per million, and it tells you a lot about how they respect law and order. In marked contrast is the United States where the latest statistics show 6.9 murders per 100,000 people in 2021 (see chart), equivalent to 69 killings per million, about 40 times higher than the Egyptian rate.

## U.S. murder rate

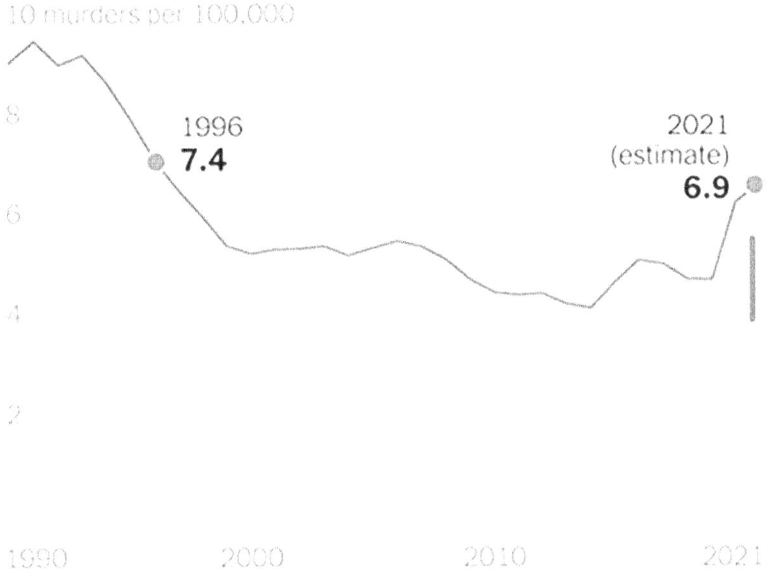


In this adopted stance within Biblical context capital punishment is the only real deterrent to murder since the killer fears being killed, and in premeditated cases this stops him. God gave us this eye for an eye system for good reason 3500 years ago, to purge the evil from amongst society. Exodus 21:23-25 (NAS) tells us "…you shall appoint as a penalty life for life, eye for eye, tooth for tooth, hand for hand…" Not following this means continually building more prisons and imposing higher taxes to pay for keeping the criminals comfortable. Who speaks for the families of the murdered- those who are condemned to spend the rest of their lives brokenhearted, left feeling there was no justice for their slain loved ones when the killer is free to live his life; meanwhile their murdered loved one lies in the ground.

Remember the heart of man is desperately wicked (Jeremiah 17:9 NAS), and therefore God's prescription for crime is even, although soft headed judges will allow the murderers to live back amongst us after a few years or less in jail. 60%+ of criminals re-commit at least one crime after release, and murderers kill again, so letting them out is not acceptable. These lenient judges say "if we enact the death penalty we are no better than the killer," but they are redefining the law that God already gave us long ago, replacing God's will with their own. Whether a judge believes in God or not, lenient penalties for crime result in a breakdown of society: criminals have a field day every day while lawful citizens are unable to go out safely in public. As each generation passes it becomes worse and worse until the country may be so weakened it may begin to dissolve by acts of civil war, continuous mass killings, invasion, or may be given over and overtaken by another country more disciplined in crime and justice, however unforeseen these barbaric scenarios may ensue.

*"There is a way that seems right to a person, but its end is the way of death"* – Proverbs 14:12 NAS

Another prevalent argument against capital punishment results from a fundamental misunderstanding of the teachings of Jesus, who stated in Matthew 5:17 (NAS) "Do not presume that I came to abolish the Law or the Prophets; I did not come to abolish, but to fulfill." During this teaching when He famously says to turn the other cheek Jesus is advising to de-escalate an argument before it turns into a violent altercation. He is saying to not over react, but he's not saying to allow someone to break your jaw or take out your eye. The Mosaic "eye for an eye" laws at the time of Jesus were in place; thus, Jesus is attempting to maintain peace before a reaction turns into a more serious event where the Mosaic law becomes involved. If you can walk away by controlling your anger that is better than everyone involved going through a protracted legal court case, and a bloody penalty decided against the perpetrator.

Some people in modern society would say punishment for crime is racist, but how can it be racist when the people disproportionately incarcerated are the same race of people whose neighborhoods by far are affected the most with crime? One would have to include many more complex and possible causative variables to justify or refute this argument, but basically God's way works, man's does not. A dead victim is a final outcome and no amount of racial equality can ever bring him back. Everyone has the basic right to be safe regardless of race. Safety first.

Moreover, it is unnatural to be so concerned with helping the criminal over the peaceful law-abiding citizen so much that the good people get killed- this is a perversion of justice, and has nothing to do with what Jesus taught.

I realize this is more than an intense subject for most people, and am not trying to give a comprehensive study on the subject of crime or punishment. This is to bring God's view into focus and present His will on the matter by providing a snapshot of two very different perspectives.

# CHAPTER 3

## The Hands

Joshua Martin or as everyone calls him Josh, grew up in Silverton, New Jersey in Ocean County on the Jersey shoreline and lived in a community focused on appreciating and living with the ocean and all the magnificence that it offered. When he was fourteen his parents opened a small curio shop on the boardwalk in Seaside Heights, and Josh worked there in the summers cleaning, stocking and taking inventory and whatever else his dad prompted him to do. They would take the eastward drive on Route 37 to get there where life was good and very fun, and where Josh could never be bored since entertainment was at his fingertips. The boardwalk had a small amusement park he and his friends frequented when he earned enough money to buy rides.

Even just walking along the boardwalk was enough to engulf the mind in never ending stimulations from the constant entourage of tourists passing by. One could be curious about the world so much because after all it was always right there happening in front of you. There's an air of smugness that develops among beach kids that know they are a privileged group, a sort of snobbery that manifests through realizing those who live further into the mainland want what you have. Teenagers can get conceited because they haven't lived long enough to know the importance of being humble. When you are young your body is strong, you feel invincible and you are not prone to even examining the possibility of weakness: it's all about acceptance among your peers, strength of friendships and seizing any experience that provides fun.

They spent the summer months in this exciting place so much that the time passed quickly, which is always the case when you are happy in life. In their junior year in high school he and his best buddy Terry Thiel would get strenuous workouts by swimming around the North Pier in Barnegat Bay, just four blocks west of his parent's shop and away from the tourist crowds at the boardwalk. Both boys were avid and capable swimmers having grown up in ocean towns. After breakfast they started their day in this way, loving the exhilarating push required of their bodies to swim completely around the pier.

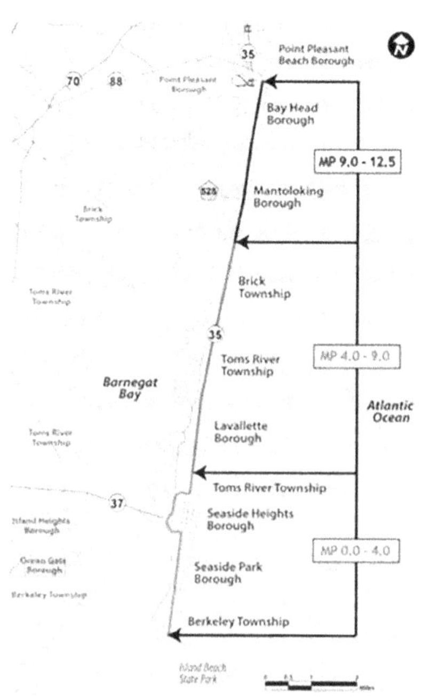

In mid-August Terry and two girls from the high school drill team wanted to drive up to Brick beach. This is an area along the strand that has less crowds and a takeout café for sodas and sandwiches. On a bright sunny day with just the right amount of clouds, Terry drove Josh and the girls five miles north, so scenic and fresh up Route 35.

They all went in the sea for a quick splash to cool off before the girls sat partially under umbrellas with their legs in the sun to get a tan. Josh bought everyone cokes and nachos and as they sat eating Terry said he wanted to go for a swim. A hurricane had swept by four days ago and a red flag had been out a few days earlier, but the waves didn't look dangerous today thought Josh. The waves were only at four feet, ideal for some body surfing so Terry convinced the girls Connie and Susan to learn how to body surf. "No you go ahead" said Susan, but Connie urged her to try "C'mon I want to learn this" she implored. So they all went in and after a few tries easily caught the waves, their bodies riding them in with great fun. Body surfing is really a blast because the wave is doing all the work and you are literally going with the flow. To catch a wave they had to go out seventy-five yards, which is not too far out from the shore. You wait as one rolls toward you, then when it's almost upon you swim like heck with all you have to catch it. You'll be one with the wave riding it as it brings you toward the shore or sideways for a while. After ten minutes of swim time Connie and Terry walked along the shore, the small waves lapping gently on their ankles as they played at splashing and laughing.

Presently Connie and Susan came to sit under the umbrellas together again to continue their leg tanning session and Terry joined them. Terry was interested in Connie and she had brought Susan along to even out the outing but Josh wasn't particularly attracted to her, although he did make an effort to be nice. Josh stayed in the water and thought he would maybe dive and search for some shells. If he found some he could give them to Susan.

He was about a hundred fifty yards out to sea now and noticed the current was powerful and large, not moving inward so much, drawing him further out. So far nothing in the power of the ocean that he couldn't handle, so he swam with a wave to catch it toward shore but instead of riding it the wave decided to bring him downward, so he swam up to get a huge breath before water engulfed him again. He was treading water and tried again to ride the wave by body surfing but they were rolling and controlling, not breaking to any degree where he could manage through them. He was being taken further and further out and realized this was a rip tide that had seized him. However, Josh felt he could out swim it by going sideways and so stopped trying to get to shore, swimming parallel to it trying to get out of the full force of the rip current. Suddenly a huge wave slammed him down to the bottom where he saw the golden sand bar right in front of his face. He didn't panic, just used his legs to push off the sand to the surface where he took a big breath of air before another wave dragged him under again. Now danger encircled his life and he fought to get to the surface but every time he got a gulp of air it wasn't enough and so became less and less able as he struggled to survive. The rip tide pulled him out two hundred yards from shore now and far from his friends who had no idea what was happening.

There were no life guards on duty that day so Josh was on his own. Again another slam down to the bottom and he pushed himself up by his legs but could not get to the surface. He thought "this can't be happening I can do this" and tried in vain for air. He saw the golden sand at the bottom of the ocean again, still cognizant but losing awareness. He swallowed a gulp of water and knew this was a very bad thing, and with his last thought said in his mind "God please help me."

*"The snares of death encompassed me, and the terrors of the netherworld came upon me."* -Psalm 116:3 (NAS)

He had no breath left when a pair of mighty hands gripped under his arm pits and he felt his body shooting quickly to the surface. He arrived above water gasping for air and immediately resumed swimming sideways out of the rip current, for he knew that was his only chance. Josh swam for fifty or more yards parallel to the shore before he was able to turn and get back onto the beach. When the ebb was at his knees and he was safely standing he looked out at the sea for who it was that saved his life. Josh assumed it was a life guard but none were there; indeed no one was in the ocean swimming at all at that time. The only thing in the water were a couple of single masted sailboats, but they were off in the distance too far to have helped him. He was incredulous, breathing hard, his eyes scanning for someone there who he could report to send out help for. He realized now with full awareness that someone had pulled him up from the bottom but could not see anyone there. He stood for a few minutes searching for something that had to be there before walking back to his friends. Josh kept stopping and looking, his eyes peering out toward the sea for anyone who was in danger swimming out there, for the person who had been there for him in his ill-fated moment. No one in sight.

Ten minutes later he was back with the group. "Hey what happened?" said Terry. "Don't go in, there's a rip tide- it got me -it's really strong" warned Josh. "Whoa dude, we were wondering where you were" Terry exclaimed. Josh sat down and told them what happened and how he felt someone grab him and take him to the surface. "There must be someone out there" Connie said "we should report this he might need help" she urged. "I looked for a long time and never saw anyone there" Josh told her. Terry got up and walked a few feet away and called 911. He explained what had happened to the medical personnel before returning to where the others sat listening. "They're checking to see if anyone is working here today" informed Terry. Josh was still shaken after the experience and sat quietly for the rest of the outing at the beach while his friends gabbed on about school and their friends.

The incident replayed in his mind over and over as he tried to identify who or what had saved him from the deadly rip current. He remembered attending church once as a young kid with his parents when a distant uncle had passed away but had no real understanding of God. He said in his mind a thank-you to God; after all he was so very glad to be alive after his brush with death. He decided he wanted to understand more and felt maybe this wasn't his time to die, that there was something in life he could do to make the world better before leaving it. He had always felt invincible and now knew this was not the case; there are much more powerful forces in our lives that we are not in control of.

*"Gracious is the LORD, and righteous; Yes, our God is compassionate. The LORD watches over the simple; I was brought low, and He saved me." -Psalm 116:5-6 (NAS)*

This was a humbling experience for Joshua Martin, to say the least. He gained a new curiosity and respect for God because he realized that this had been no ordinary event, that something supernatural had intervened in his life. He began to grow up that day and his attitude changed. He even started to treat people around him with more consideration and understanding because he was grateful to be alive every day and wanted to be worthy of life.

Joshua Martin was seventeen in 2019 when he survived this incident. At the time of this writing he is in college studying to be a civil engineer, with an emphasis on coastal engineering. Since the east coast erodes beachfront while the west coast accumulates it, Josh has expressed he is interested in techniques that prevent erosion of the eastern coastline.

Some may be skeptical to accept that Josh was saved in the middle of the ocean, not thinking it could be possible. However, God is everywhere and his four elements are of the earth itself: water, fire, rock and wind. In Psalm 24:1 (NAS) we see the earth belongs to God:

*"The earth is the Lord's, and all it contains, the world, and those who live in it. For He has founded it upon the seas and established it upon the rivers."*

What it supernatural to us is perfectly natural to God who basically speaks things into existence. Yes, by merely speaking it, as shown in the book of Genesis His words become the reality of the earth.

# He Gave Back to His Community

*"Be constantly alert, and strengthen the things that remain"*

-Revelation 3:2 (NAS)

In this passage there is an implied message that we are to value what is worthy of our support or those things may not be there too long if we don't. Once again we come to the struggle between free will and fate. You see, if you do not take action to push back on evil it will gain power. If you continue to do nothing it takes over- this is called fate. An example would be if a person merely sits on his sofa day after day and doesn't work or pay rent, fate takes over and soon the authorities come to his door evicting and removing him. To avoid fate take action to preserve your freedom, for there are always people within institutions who seek power and will gladly take your freedom away from you.

Why strengthen those things that are good- because we know that bad things can happen to good people, so if you can prevent calamity it is a good thing. People ask why does God allow calamity and evil but it is man who does evil works, and this causes God to pull away from those who are not in His will. Soon after He holds back His protection evil occurs.

Here on earth life is a mixture of good and evil. It's important for us to figure this out and use our faculty of moral equivalency, or discernment so we can choose good over evil while you can. Friendship and love have long range effects on the human soul and they cause an evolution toward God.

In the universe we see everything is changing and there is no real permanence. To an atheist his absolute truth may be that there is no absolute truth. That is impossible to defend since the person saying there is no absolute truth is using that very statement as their absolute truth; in effect this cancels out their own argument, leaving no solid ground to stand on, no starting point to begin rational thinking.

People are naturally self-centered when they don't have God. Left to their own devices it will be like the time in Judges 21:25 (NAS) when "In those days there was no king in Israel; everyone did what was right in his own eyes." Without moral guidance it's easy to descend into an animalistic type of behavior: for example, looking to take from your neighbor instead of creating or supplying good things for yourself. This is the opposite of what Jesus said about how to behave: "In everything, therefore, treat people the same way you want them to treat you, for this is the Law and the Prophets." (Matthew 7:12 & Luke 6:31, NAS) This is also known as the Golden Rule of life. Joshua Martin chose an occupation where he was not only thinking about himself but the world at large.

Finally, God is not subject to our logic; he has his own opinions and doesn't bend for us, so we could try to understand what he wants. He is the spirit who creates life and resides in heaven. We on earth have no power to restore life and since we cannot bring back the dead to life as Jesus did, we have no right to take life away. This coupled with the previous axiom of the Golden Rule provides a balanced, existential perspective that promotes respect for yourself and others.

The great unknown...there are so many things we don't know we can't tackle them all, so focusing on one thing at a time is easier; this is how most of us function. However, the variants in the world work simultaneous to each other and nothing is occurring in a vacuum. Motion, space and time happen together in a continuum.

So looking at history, science and the present together might help to gain understanding of what is going on and in what direction things are moving; howbeit that it doesn't tell us why things are as they are, it merely shows superficial causes and effects which are not always closely related in time.

Calvinism says God is in control of everything, and that all His predictions will eventually come true. Looking at life this way makes it seem like we are in a closed system whose outcome has already been decided for us. God will do what He says he'll do, yes, but you always have choices. The element of free will must always be considered because that is part of what we have going for us. The things we are often not aware off are the consequences of our choices, and that is why we need understanding.

# CHAPTER 4

## The In-Between Dream

Shannon was seventeen in 2018 when she went to a rock concert at the TCU Amphitheater at the White River State Park in downtown Indianapolis. She and her boyfriend Billy with their two friends sat in the back area on the lawn under the stars on a clear night and became one with the young energetic crowd, swaying to the exhilaratingly loud beat of each of the three bands they heard that night. They had brought some beer with them and easily finished the six pack. Someone next to them was passing around a joint of marijuana, and Billy toked on it without hesitation: "Thanks man," Billy said to the teen next to him, then passed it to Shannon. She was gazing at the electric lights coming out from the stage, lights that stopped in front of them in the shape of floating squares. "Huh I wonder how they do that?" she asked Billy, who was smiling and singing along with the words to a popular song. "They do it with lasers" Billy said.

After the concert Billy, Shannon and their friends Mark and Carrie walked to Billy's van together, the walk slightly sobering them up, for they had to remember where Billy had parked. Presently they piled in, Mark and Carrie in the back seat, Shannon in the front with Billy.

"That was knarly dude" said Mark "thanks a lot, cool." "Yeah, pretty radical" replied Billy who started the van and put on some music. Six miles later on 38th Street going toward Mark's house on Meridian Street Carrie was already asleep and so was Shannon who had been fighting the sleepiness, but due to the effects of the alcohol and marijuana couldn't help herself and so slumped onto the window.

They were driving along 38th Street about half a mile from Mark's house, going about fifty miles an hour when Billy caught himself dozing off, his head jerking sharply upward, ran over the curb, hit the brakes and swerved the van with a hard turn to the left causing it to careen with a wobble. Losing control, Billy tried to compensate with a sharp turn to the right, but this made the van bounce on its right side once with an impact that caused the passenger door to burst open. That bounce was so hard the van turned upright again, the entire right side badly damaged. Shannon was tossed out of the van like a rag doll, first feeling her body slam around inside before flying out onto the pavement.

Shannon lay on the side of the road with a major concussion, while the other three teens suffered injuries that ranged from Carrie's broken arm to Mark's crushed left knee. It appeared Billy was the only one who had no major injuries.

There was a small structure twenty yards away just inside a gate and the security guard who worked there heard the van scrape on the road, looked out the window and called 911 for help. He then ran out to try to help anyone who might be injured. Mark and Carrie sat in the back dazed and slowly became cognizant of what had just happened. Billy got to Shannon's side and started to pick her up but the security guard whose name said "Dan" on his shirt warned "It's not a good idea to move her-you might cause more damage than if you just leave her alone. I called 911 and they're coming." Security guard Dan rolled up his jacket and very gingerly placed it under Shannon's head.

Shannon fought to wake up but her brain kept rolling in and out of the scene and she could not distinguish if this was reality or a dream. Her adrenaline started pumping and part of her mind realized the awful event that had transpired, but the alcohol and pot took a toll on her sensibilities. Passing out she had a dream she was walking then sort of floating a few feet off the ground through rows of headstones. Hundreds of headstones lined a huge stretch of land and bright moonlight shone on them all. Shannon did not know where she was and for a moment thought she was back at the concert or some entertainment venue because there were all sorts of people sitting on the stones and statues, people sitting on the ground next to them and one small group of middle-aged people were actually having a picnic on a parcel of ground she passed by! Only about a third of the headstones were abandoned with no one representing them. In front of her there was a plump older couple sitting on top of their stones, smiling cheerfully as she went by. "Hello welcome" the man greeted, as the lady turned to the man and said "Stan I don't think she's staying."

Shannon kept walking, now creeped out and wanting an exit out of there, but every time she thought there was an exit she moved toward, the rows just kept going on and on. She couldn't seem to leave and was becoming frustrated. "I'll go back the way I came" she thought and started back along the main walkway. She was instantly at the side entrance where apparently she had come in. To her amazement her cousin Frank was standing there in front of her in the driveway, his eyes an intense expression of love and urgency. At twenty-one years of age Frank had been killed in a rappelling accident in Yosemite, California last fall when his harness strap had failed him causing him to slip out and plummet several stories down the side of the rock face he was climbing. Investigators said later that the tied knot was not the right kind of knot for rappelling and somehow had become undone. Shannon remembered that she and Frank were close as children, often being paired together at family get togethers where Frank always looked after her, for he was a few years older. She loved him and losing him was so very painful she still had not really let go. "Frank I miss you" she implored.

Frank pointed to the sky and said "Look they're coming." Shannon looked up and saw a pair of angels circling ten yards above them. The angels were a male and a female in their mid-twenties, the slim dark haired male wearing jeans and a blue shirt, the pretty blond female wearing a lacey gossamer style dress. They were beautiful and intelligent looking with fiery eyes that bore through your soul when they looked at you. They had a pleasant yet fearless expression and when her eyes met the female's eyes Shannon felt as though this angel knew all about her even though they had never met before. The angels came lower, the female lower still to get a closer look at Shannon while the male remained circling watching from above. As the angels drew closer to Frank the vision ended and Shannon gained consciousness.

Angels have always been a symbol of those who gather souls, whether to heaven (Matthew 24:31) or to hell (Matthew 13:41-43). Early in God's word they appeared when Jacob saw a ladder to heaven: "And he had a dream, and behold, a ladder was set up…And behold, the angels of God were ascending and descending on it." (Genesis 28:12 NAS) Had these angels come for Frank?

Awakening, she became aware again of the van accident and was lying flat on a hard patient transport unit about four feet off the ground, carried by two Emergency Medical Technicians. There was a police car to the left and an officer standing near the road as if to watch for traffic. She was taped to the stretcher so it was hard to turn her head, but when she did turn it to the right thirty degrees her eyes saw the entrance to a cemetery. "Am I dead?" she asked the medical responders. "No mam" replied the older paramedic "we're taking care of you, now just keep still and let us do our job" he said. She could see Billy standing close by who pleaded "Shannon Babe I'm so sorry. You're gonna make it you'll be all right." The EMT waved Billy back saying there would be time for this later not now. Her head really hurt bad with a hard pounding sound that wouldn't stop so she couldn't acknowledge Billy anyway.

A second ambulance approached for Mark and Carrie who were helped in. While Shannon was in the first ambulance moving fast to the hospital they gave her morphine for the pain, and this made her pass out again. This time there was no sensation, no dreams just nothingness.

She awoke in the Intensive Care Unit of the IU Health Methodist Hospital three miles away from the accident location which she learned was the Crown Hill Cemetery. Standing a few feet from her bed were her parents who came right over to her side when they saw her open her eyes. Her father said "We got a call this morning and hurried over, on account of they said they didn't know if you would die or be all right." A doctor came in and told

Shannon she had a concussion but no fracture, so the prognosis was good. Her Mom and Dad half smiled and Dad said Shannon was so hard headed probably nothing could crack it anyway. Mom held her hand and said they loved her and would take care of her and make sure she was all right. Dad said not to worry about anything, just take it easy for a while and get better. The Doctor informed that the impact had been on the upper left cranium resulting in a traumatic brain injury. Shannon's head had been slammed hard then dragged for a few feet and some brain cells had been destroyed. The left side of her body was scraped up and bloody. However, healing was imminent and due to her young age Shannon was going to be fine in a few weeks.

After her parents left it was a long day of sleep. That evening Shannon thought about the dream and remembered that during it she had not even realized she was in a cemetery! The more she thought about it the more amazed she was about the experience. That dream was lucid and she had felt awake in it even more than she was now. So many details were crystal clear, especially those precious few moments with Frank. She had never had an altered state of consciousness like that before and now realized that those were tombstones with the dead who were buried there hanging around them. The loss of Frank had been a pain in her heart, but as she lay recovering sensed there was closure in that he had come to say goodbye. Those beautiful angels had come for him.

A part of Shannon was still getting over the shock from the terrible accident, and she decided a change had to be made. As the horrific events replayed over and over in her mind she decided to never allow anything like that to happen again. Shannon made a decision to not drink alcohol anymore because she realized that and the marijuana were the factors that led to Billy falling asleep at the wheel. Sadly, her love for Billy was fading fast, replaced by a sort of resentment that his carelessness had almost cost her everything. Shannon didn't hate Billy, she was just majorly annoyed at him. Even more she was annoyed at herself, feeling partially responsible for allowing him to drive intoxicated. She felt stupid and was hugely disappointed with herself for taking substances that dulled her state of mind, and that led to poor decisions. You only have one body, one life and she almost lost hers.

*1 Corinthians 6:19 (NAS) tells us "…your body is a temple of the Holy Spirit within you, whom you have from God…"* Shannon wanted to turn away from substance abuse and have a clear head and be her natural self, not always addicted to alcohol and marijuana. If she didn't, next time she might not be lucky enough to survive, and the dream was a warning of how close she came to death. Very close. She decided there would be no next time. Why were certain souls forgotten, left on earth she wondered- well, at least they didn't go to the bad place, but being earth bound isn't the ideal either. Angels came for Frank who had been a believer in God but he hadn't gone to church regularly. She was paired with him during family weddings and baptisms in churches and they had prayed together, and he had been a decent guy who never committed crimes. Frank loved the beauty of the earth and was an outdoor type. He had sent out many pictures of the sunset to her through his cell phone. "I think he'll be all right" Shannon thought. "Thank you God for not letting me die," then she drifted off to sleep again.

The staff in the intensive care unit would not allow anyone other than immediate family to visit her, so when Billy tried he was not let in. She asked for her phone and saw that he had left text messages for her apologizing for the accident and that he wanted to see her. She texted him back that she was not ready to see him and that she needed time to heal, but deep inside she knew their relationship was over.

During Shannon's near-death experience while she lay unconscious to the physical world her soul existed somewhere in between life and death. As she was viewing a macabre portion of the netherworld at the graveyard it became an opportune vehicle for her beloved cousin Frank to say goodbye. The presence of benevolent angels showed that God cared and was there, as He is an omnipresent spirit, and those particular beings were working in those moments for Shannon and Frank's spiritual benefit.

*"Where can I go from Your Spirit? Or where can I flee from Your presence? If I ascend to heaven, You are there; If I make my bed in Sheol, behold, You are there."*

-Psalm 139:7-8 (NAS)

Shannon was not quite in Sheol or Hell, but still in some facsimile of an earthly realm, where she witnessed earth bound spirits lingering in a graveyard. Somehow the power of her love helped witness Frank's departure for heaven.

# Shannon's Spiritual Experience

If you'd like the world to make sense then objective truth and logic are for you. The science-leaning philosophical side of Biblical Parapsychology is not subjective or emotional, rather it is measured by empirical evidence that you see in front of you. Therefore, it has nothing to do with opinions, only the reality of things just as they are; with that being said, biblical passages are then aligned with those realities. What we know about things is how they appear because we see them. To discern something hidden requires serious contemplation and the Bible helps with that; thus, we include subjective thought mixed with objective thought based on all levels of perception.

We know typically we have five senses while awake: sight, hearing, touch, taste and smell. However, we can only perceive a small portion of the electromagnetic spectrum, yet x-rays, gamma rays and many more invisible energies exist, so our senses are only reliable to their natural limits. Therefore, could there be that we have a sixth sense that is not readily apparent but occasionally shows itself to us?

One may ponder the various characters of souls apart from their bodies: why do some seem to be angels, and others like ghouls or phantoms? Who decides all that and on what basis? Certainly we don't have the power of judgement, and that is where God comes in.

There is good and there is evil- this is objective reality, for if your eyes are open you do see that in your everyday lives. However, the degree on which you judge what those things are depends on the individual subjective choices you make. If your mind and heart do not seek the truth you may have already opened the door, or given license to evil. "…because they did not accept the love of truth so as to be saved. For this reason God will send upon them a deluding influence so that they will believe what is false…" (2 Thessalonians 2:11, New American Standard). Here, it looks like God does not have infinite patience for those who do not respect truth; instead He curses those who do not turn to the truth.

Honest assessment is necessary for a free society: why, because without honesty you will get lies and tyranny, and with those things death follows. Choose life, choose what is good and true and you will be free. With freedom comes happiness.

One philosopher who spent a great deal of contemplative energy on the abstract subject of existence relative to the afterlife was Plato. In his Theory of Forms [1] he purports that ultimate reality exists beyond our physical world. The Realm of Forms is the spiritual realm, sort of an ancient Greek parallel to heaven, where our physical world here can never be as real or true as the spiritual world there because the spiritual contains the essences and qualities of perfection in and of those forms. Plato says there is a duality of existence, the physical and the spiritual, and the physical world is but a shadow of true reality which exists in the forms. When your soul is finally released from your body you get to exist in a perfect spiritual world. This sounds too convenient until you apply the axiom that Jesus's blood bought you an afterlife.

Plato says these forms are already perfect. However, could it be that we are in a constant state of evolution striving towards perfection, where we participate through our physical lives in shaping that perfection by taking the good qualities with us when we physically pass away and continue into the spiritual realm? This theory gives a purpose for our existence and value to our souls, in that through all our trials and tribulations if we choose rightly we are becoming better and closer to God who is the only perfect being. Plato may be partially describing heaven, but not the means how to get there. The spiritual realm might be improving and becoming more perfect as souls pass into it. We call it perfect as that's all we know of it at the moment because its transitivity is unbeknown to us.

This theorem can be expressed thus:

A= soul of a good person who brings a measurement of perfection

B= now state of perfect heaven

C= a more perfect heaven

$$A+B=C \qquad \text{therefore, } C > B$$

*"For this perishable must put on the imperishable, and this mortal must put on immortality."* -1 Corinthians 15:53 (NAS)

In this passage we see that God has made us with an immortal soul. According to the law of thermodynamics energy cannot be created or destroyed, it only converts to another form. To this day no one has been able to obtain a material sample of the energy of a soul for analysis, other than a white, powdery substance called ectoplasm, and there has been no conclusive analysis of that yet.

During Shannon's near-death experience she was in a state of altered consciousness. We normally don't see a side of death as she did, nor do we know of all the places and dimensions where our souls can go. God is a multi-dimensional spirit, the one who created these places where souls travel to. It stands to reason that He also created our souls as well to inhabit them: why build a house if no one is going to live in it?

When Jesus Christ died in the flesh, His spirit continued working for our benefit. By traveling to the paradise area of hell or Sheol, He brought the saved into ascension by rescuing them from there.

Even before Jesus's physical body was crucified He had predicted to His disciples in Matthew 12:40 (NAS) "for just as Jonah was in the stomach of the sea monster for three days and three nights, so will the Son of Man be in the heart of the earth for three days and three nights." So that's where he was at least for some of those three days before He came back to town.

Hell could not hold the Messiah, who tells us in Revelation 1:18 (NAS) that He holds the keys to death and hell: "I was dead, and behold, I am alive forevermore, and I have the keys of death and of Hades." If someone holds keys to a door or gate that would mean that passageway is necessarily locked, otherwise there would be no need for a key- this implies a finality that was not there before Christ interceded. Hence, one must have faith in the Messiah to gain a good life after death. Whether that spiritual life is in heaven or hell, Jesus is in charge of the judgement: "For just as the Father has life in Himself, so He gave to the Son also to have life in Himself; and He gave Him authority to execute judgment, because He is the Son of Man." (John 5:26-27 NAS)

At the moment when Jesus died on the cross, the temple curtain ripped in two, an earthquake occurred, and tombs opened. A curious simultaneity when Jesus exited the tomb after the three days was that these "holy ones" who also came out of their tombs were walking around the city (Matthew 27:51-53 NAS). The Bible does not go on to tell us what happened to those souls after they had "appeared to many."

Psalm 16:10 (NAS) tells us "For You will not abandon my soul to Sheol; You will not allow Your Holy One to undergo decay." This is Jesus speaking to God the father about His bodily resurrection, and indeed later the apostles did witness His bodily ascension from the Mount of Olives on the fortieth day of His spiritual-bodily resurrection. (Acts 1:9 NAS).

1. *Plato, The Republic, Theory of Forms, circa 420-340 BC*

# ABOUT THE AUTHOR

The author is a researcher, an advisor, a statistician, a legislative analyst, a mountain climber, a fencer, an actor, a teacher, a photographer, a program designer for gifted programs, new teacher training, literacy groups and testing outcomes. She has worked as an External Evaluator in the California's Underperforming Schools Program (IIUSP). She holds an A.A. degree, a B.A. degree and a M.S. degree, and others.

Ms. Raleigh has designed four instruction models for the Los Angeles Unified School District, all copyrighted in 1997, while at Eagle Rock High School. She has won a Certificate of Recognition award from the LAUSD Board for "Survival," the best Senior High Standards-Based Instruction Model, but evidently the most popular model was the one called "Transcendentalism," sparking a modern revival of the American Transcendentalist movement which has its fundamental roots in Emerson, Thoreau and Whitman, all of whose works are used in the model. Other teaching models are "Etymology," that provides a study in word origins, and "Literal and Implied Meanings," that explores societal perceptions of gender. Copies of the models are available upon request sent to the P.O. Box address below.

The author has invented a way to improve reading comprehension, and the research paper has been published by The Educational Resources Information Center (ERIC), the U.S. Department of Education office website. First published as "A Constructivist Technique Which Improves Reading Comprehension," SP 038 687, the paper has been updated into modern terms and is now copyrighted as "Using Emotional Intelligence to Improve Reading Comprehension," in 2016. Copies are available by request to the P.O. Box address below.

While working on the language designs of the California Standards Ms. Raleigh was an Associate Director at the UCLA School Management Program under Director Charlotte Higuchi of Center X.

She has designed four multi-cultural classes in conjunction with the J. Paul Getty Museum, the Huntington Museum and the Japanese American Museum from 1995 through 1999. The Japanese American Museum class was held on March 15, 1997, and included a presentation followed by a book signing by Jeanne Wakatsuki Houston, the author of Farewell to Manzanar.

If the reader has any questions about the availability of contents of this manuscript please write to the author at P.O. Box 331, Cody, Wyoming, 82414